Oxford International Primary History

Workbook

6

Peter Rebman

Oxford International Primary for enquiring minds

Great Clarendon Street, Oxford, OX2 6DP, United Kingdom

Oxford University Press is a department of the University of Oxford. It furthers the University's objective of excellence in research, scholarship, and education by publishing worldwide. Oxford is a registered trade mark of Oxford University Press in the UK and in certain other countries.

The moral rights of the author have been asserted.

First published in 2017

All rights reserved. No part of this publication may be reproduced, stored in a retrieval system, or transmitted, in any form or by any means, without the prior permission in writing of Oxford University Press, or as expressly permitted by law, by licence or under terms agreed with the appropriate reprographics rights organization. Enquiries concerning reproduction outside the scope of the above should be sent to the Rights Department, Oxford University Press, at the address above.

You must not circulate this work in any other form and you must impose this same condition on any acquirer.

British Library Cataloguing in Publication Data
Data available

ISBN: 978-0-19-841820-7

12

Paper used in the production of this book is a natural, recyclable product made from wood grown in sustainable forests. The manufacturing process conforms to the environmental regulations of the country of origin.

Printed in India by Multivista Global Pvt. Ltd.

Acknowledgements

Cover illustration: Carlo Molinari/Advocate Arti

Illustrations: Aptara

Photos: p5 & p17 & 72: The Sea Warriors (gouache on paper), English School, (20th century)/Private Collection/© Look and Learn/Bridgeman Images; **p11 (T):** Werner Forman/Getty; **p11 (B):** Werner Forman/Getty; **p14:** robertharding/Alamy; **p21:** The 'Pinta', the 'Nina' and the 'Santa Maria' sailing towards the West Indies in 1492, from The Discovery of America, 1878 (colour litho), Spanish School, (19th century)/Private Collection/Index/Bridgeman Images; **p28 & p68 (B):** Granger Historical Picture Archive/Alamy Stock Photo; **p32:** The Development of Printing, plate 5 from 'Nova Reperta' (New Discoveries) engraved by Philip Galle (1537-1612) c.1600 (engraving), Straet, Jan van der (Giovanni Stradano) (1523-1605) (after)/Private Collection/Bridgeman Images; **p37:** Queen Elizabeth I, 'The Ermine Portrait', 1585 (oil on panel), Hilliard, Nicholas (1547-1619) / Hatfield House, Hertfordshire, UK / Bridgeman Images; **p40:** ullstein bild/Getty; **p41 (T):** architecture UK/Alamy; **p41 (B):** Man Ploughing a Field (woodcut) (b/w photo), English School, (16th century)/Private Collection/Bridgeman Images; **p44:** Art Directors & TRIP/Alamy; **p48:** Queen Elizabeth I - The Pelican Portrait, c.1574 (oil on panel), Hilliard, Nicholas (1547-1619)/Walker Art Gallery, National Museums Liverpool/Bridgeman Images; **p49 (T):** Archivart/Alamy; **p49 (B):** Classic Image/Alamy; **p50:** Kiev.Victor/Shutterstock; **p53:** Arcaid Images/Alamy; **p55:** © Look and Learn; **p57:** Heritage Images/Getty; **p61:** World History Archive/Alamy Stock Photo; **p62 (L):** Hulton Archive/Getty; **p62 (R):** Mary Evans Picture Library; **p64 & p68 (T):** William Vandivert/Getty; **p66 & p71 (T):** Marek Stepan/Alamy; **p71 (B):** The Academy of Baccio Bandinelli, 1547 (etching), Vico, Enea (1523-1567)/Gabinetto dei Disegni e Stampe, Galleria Degli Uffizi, Florence, Italy/Bridgeman Images

Although we have made every effort to trace and contact all copyright holders before publication this has not been possible in all cases. If notified, the publisher will rectify any errors or omissions at the earliest opportunity.

Links to third party websites are provided by Oxford in good faith and for information only. Oxford disclaims any responsibility for the materials contained in any third party website referenced in this work.

The manufacturer's authorised representative in the EU for product safety is Oxford University Press España S.A. of El Parque Empresarial San Fernando de Henares, Avenida de Castilla, 2 - 28830 Madrid (www.oup.es/en or product.safety@oup.com). OUP España S.A. also acts as importer into Spain of products made by the manufacturer.

Contents

1 The Vikings

1.1	Who were the Vikings?	6
1.2	Who ruled the Vikings?	8
1.3	Farming and trade	10
1.4	The Vikings at home	12
1.5	How did the Vikings get around?	14
1.6	What achievements are the Vikings known for?	16
1	Thinking about my learning	18

2 The Age of Discovery and Exploration

2.1	Before the Age of Discovery and Exploration	22
2.2	Why was there an Age of Discovery and Exploration?	24
2.3a	Voyages of discovery and exploration	26
2.3b	Voyages of discovery and exploration	28
2.4	What was life like at sea?	30
2.5	What was the Renaissance?	32
2	Thinking about my learning	34

3 The Tudors

3.1	Who were the Tudor kings and queens?	38
3.2	Who was who in Tudor society?	40
3.3	Tudor towns	42
3.4	Fun and games in Tudor times	44
3.5	What were Tudor schools like?	46
3.6	What do Tudor portraits tell us?	48
3	Thinking about my learning	50

4 The story of London

4.1	Ancient London	54
4.2	London in the Middle Ages	56
4.3a	How did the Great Fire change London?	58
4.3b	How did the Great Fire change London?	60
4.4	The largest city in the world	62
4.5	London at war	64
4	Thinking about my learning	66

Glossary 68

1 The Vikings

What do I already know?

What do you think are good answers to the questions in the speech bubbles? Discuss your answers with some friends. Write your answers in your notebook. Your teacher will ask you to look back at your answers when you have completed the unit.

> Who were the Vikings?

> How and why did the Vikings travel?

> What did the Vikings look like?

> What was life like in a Viking village?

> What achievements are the Vikings known for?

Things I would like to know about the Vikings

_____

_____

_____

Look at this image of a Viking attack and answer the questions.

1. What impression of the Vikings do you get from this image?

   _____

   _____

2. What weapons are these Vikings using?

   _____

   _____

3. What do you think these Vikings are doing?

   _____

   _____

4. How are these Vikings dressed? What does this tell us about them?

   _____

   _____

5. How might you feel if you were one of the Vikings pictured here?

   _____

1.1 Who were the Vikings?

Where did the Vikings travel to?

1. Use your Student Book to help you colour the map and the key to show Viking settlements and raids. Use an atlas to help you label the countries.

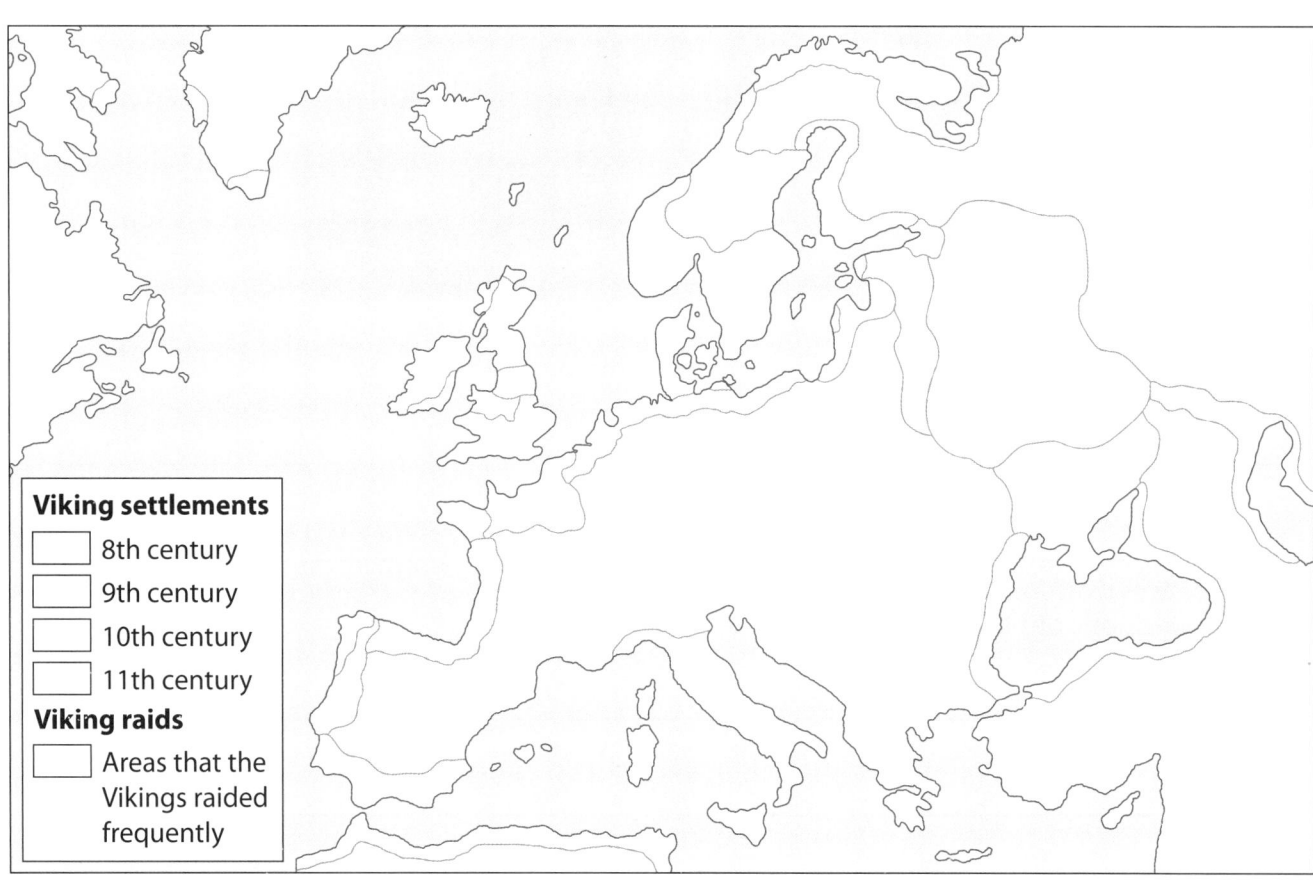

2. Why did the Vikings choose to travel to other lands?

_____

_____

_____

_____

_____

_____

Raiding, trading and exploring

1. Complete these fact cards about the Vikings. You can use the Internet or reference books for your research. Write between three and five facts in each box.

✓ **Countries the Vikings invaded**	✓ **Reasons the Vikings invaded other countries**

✓ **Jobs that Viking men and women did well**	✓ **The Vikings' achievements**

2. What do you think was the Vikings' biggest achievement? Explain your answer.

_____

_____

_____

_____

1.2 Who ruled the Vikings?

Who ruled the Vikings?

1 Complete the diagram by writing the name of each class of person.

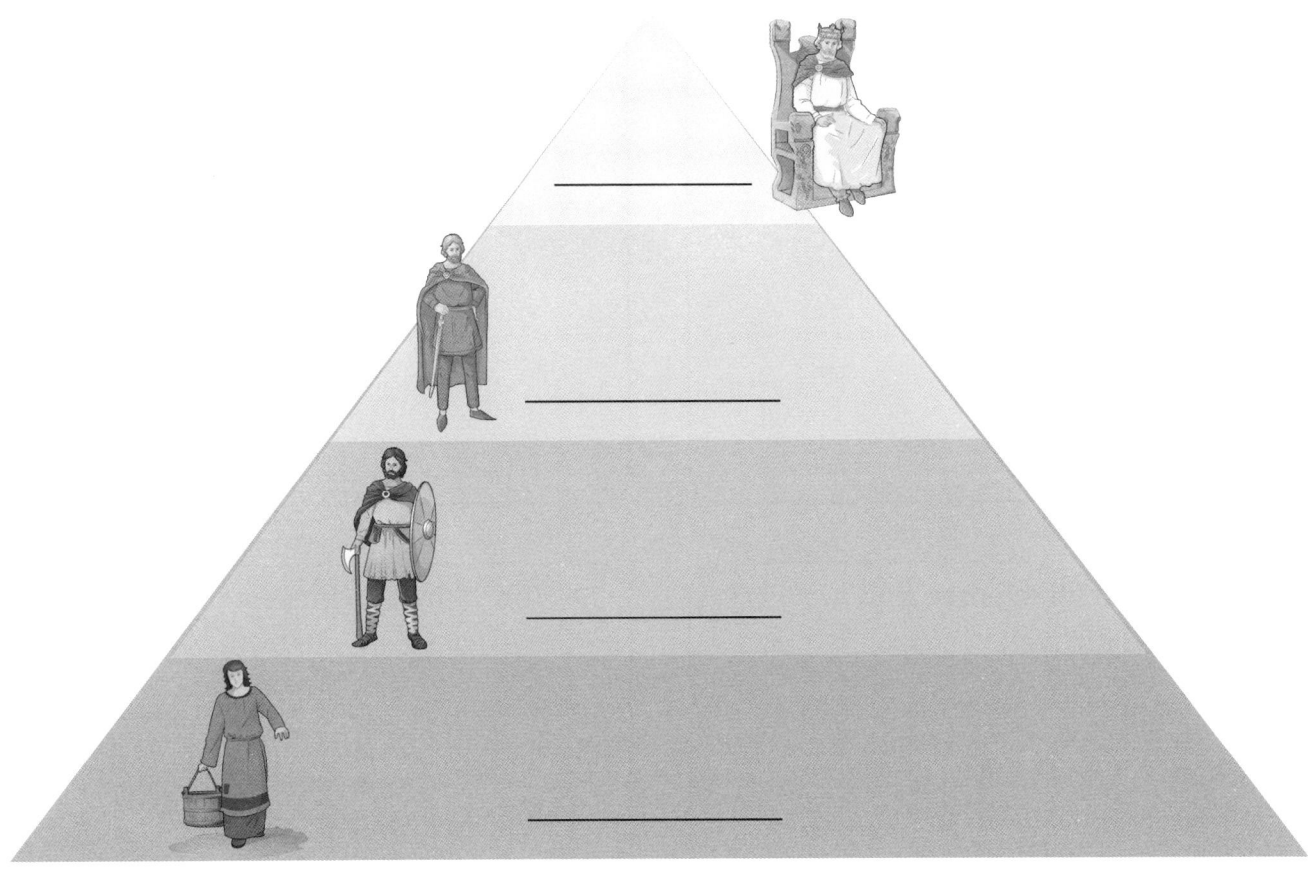

2 Why was it important for Viking society to be organised as shown in this diagram?

_____

_____

_____

3 How was a Viking child's life different from your life?

_____

_____

_____

_____

Viking profile

Create a profile for one of the classes in Viking society you have studied. Your profile will include:

- the name of the class or role
- the duties and rewards of the class or role you have chosen
- the correct key words. For example, if you write about the king, you might include words such as 'responsibility', 'protect' and 'control'. If you write about a thrall, you might include words such as 'slavery', 'loyal' and 'work'.

Name of class or role
Duties the person in this role must carry out
Benefits or rewards for carrying out these duties

1.3 Farming and trade

Farming and fishing

True or false?

1. Read the statements about Viking farming. Put ✓ in the box next to the statements that are correct. Put ✗ in the box next to the statements that are incorrect.

   a Viking farmers bought most of their food in shops. ☐

   b They grew oats, barley and wheat to make flour and porridge. ☐

   c They ate vegetables, such as aubergines and courgettes, which grew well in warm climates. ☐

   d In autumn, farmers killed some animals to provide enough food to feed their families through the winter. ☐

   e The farmland in Scandinavia was excellent and there was plenty of space to build new settlements. ☐

2. Rewrite the statements that are incorrect.

   _____

   _____

   _____

   _____

3. Write your own three statements about Viking farming and fishing. Make one or two of the statements incorrect. Ask a friend to work out which statements are true and which are false.

   _____

   _____

   _____

   _____

   _____

   _____

Using historical sources

1 What does each of these sources tell us about Viking merchants and traders?

   a Before they used coins, Viking traders carried a set of folding scales. Why did they do this?

   _____

   _____

   b This amber (fossilised tree resin) figure was part of a Viking's chess set. Where did amber come from?

   _____

   _____

   c This map shows the journeys made by Viking traders. Where did they go? Why do you think they chose to travel so far?

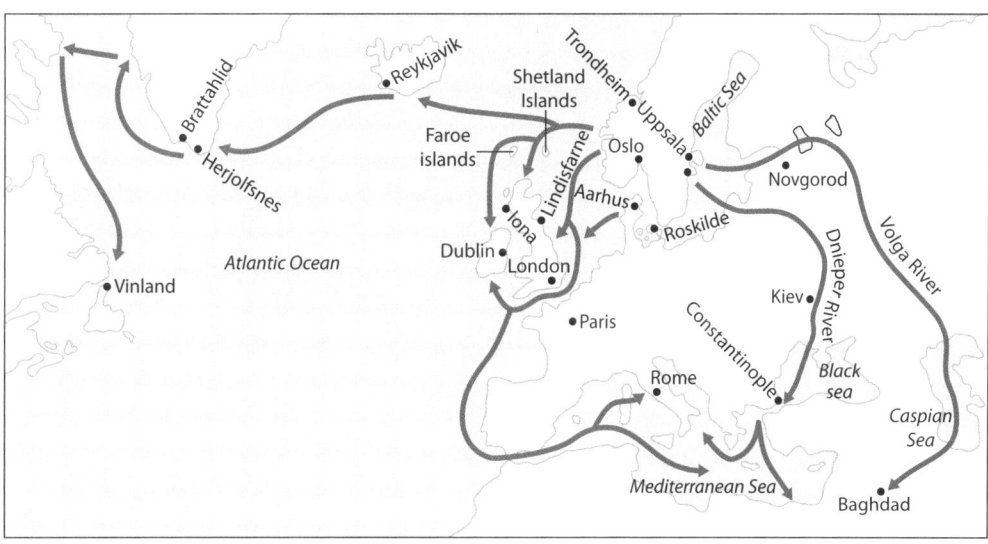

   _____

   _____

   _____

2 Why are sources like these useful for historians? Explain your answer.

   _____

   _____

1.4 The Vikings at home

Viking towns and villages

1 Look at this picture of a Viking house. Read the labels for different parts of the picture. Draw a line from each label to the correct part of the house.

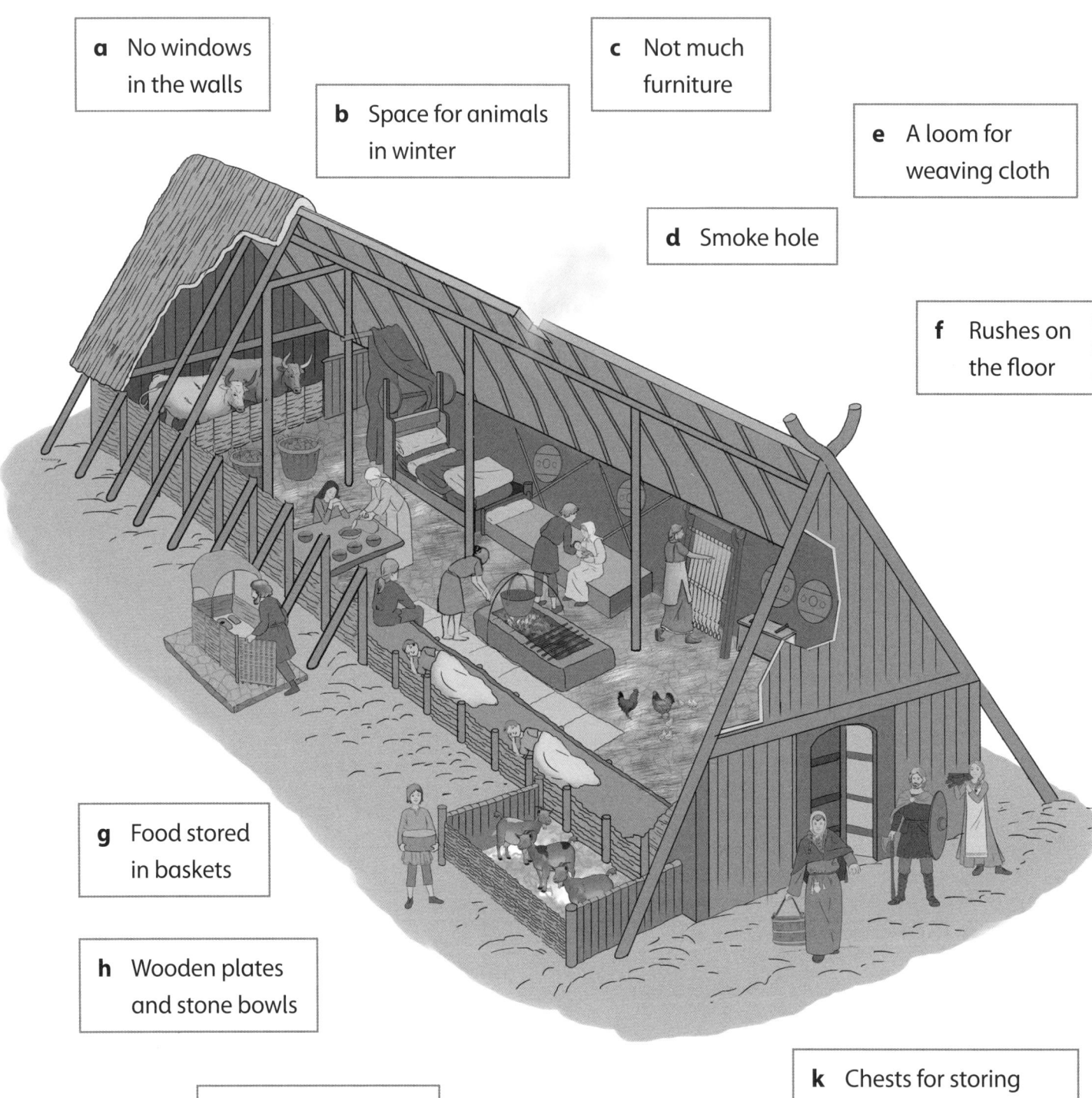

a No windows in the walls

b Space for animals in winter

c Not much furniture

d Smoke hole

e A loom for weaving cloth

f Rushes on the floor

g Food stored in baskets

h Wooden plates and stone bowls

i A fire for cooking and heat

j Many people living in one room

k Chests for storing clothes and blankets

2. Write three ways in which this Viking house is similar to your home and three ways in which it is different.

Ways in which it is similar	Ways in which it is different

My Viking diary

Imagine you are a Viking villager. Write a diary entry for a day in your life. Describe your job, your food and your house. Say whether you enjoy your life and explain why.

Dear Diary,

1.5 How did the Vikings get around?

A Viking boat

Write an advert for a Viking boat. Include a description of the boat and information about its size and speed. Explain what the boat is made from and any features it has to help the Vikings defend themselves during battle. Use reference books and the Internet to help you.

Viking boat for sale

Description

_____

_____

_____

_____

_____

_____

_____

_____

Size: _____

Speed: _____

Challenge

Write a summary in your notebook explaining how ocean travel has changed over the last 1000 years. Think about: the methods of transport that people used; the technology used to navigate and steer; the distances that people travelled in the past and now.

Viking explorers

Write an essay to describe the Vikings' travels.

The Vikings' travels

The Vikings travelled the seas using _____

_____

_____

_____

The Vikings travelled far and wide because _____

_____

_____

_____

Most of the Vikings' journeys were successful because _____

_____

_____

_____

I am/am not surprised by how far the Vikings travelled because _____

_____

_____

_____

1.6 What achievements are the Vikings known for?

Viking achievements

Here are four achievements of the Vikings.

A Craft

C Games, music and sport

B Jewellery

D Literature

Think about the importance of these achievements. Which achievement do you think had the biggest impact on people's everyday lives? Which achievement do you think did not make any real difference?

1. Use the pyramid to rank the achievements. Write the letter of the most important achievement at the top. Write the letter of the least important achievement at the bottom.

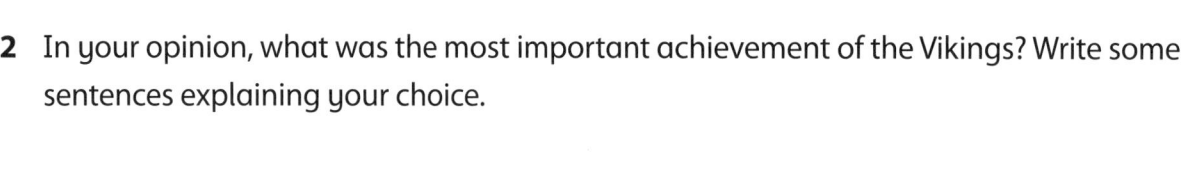

2. In your opinion, what was the most important achievement of the Vikings? Write some sentences explaining your choice.

_____

_____

_____

_____

_____

Erik the Red

The Vikings told exciting stories of adventures and Viking heroes. These stories were called sagas. The Vikings passed the sagas from one generation to the next. Research the Viking explorer Erik the Red and write a 10-line saga about his life.

Title: _____

_____

_____

_____

_____

_____

_____

_____

_____

_____

_____

Local history study

Research a famous person from the area where you live. In your notebook write a 10-line saga about the person's life or an important event from his or her history.

1 Thinking about my learning

The Vikings

Find your answers to the questions in speech bubbles on page 4 at the beginning of the unit. Use a different colour to add to your answers or rewrite them. Include any new information you have learned while studying this unit.

Chronology and change

1. Complete the table. Compare the Vikings with a group from another period of history you have studied, for example, the Romans, the Anglo-Saxons or the Maya.

	The Vikings	_____
Where did they live?		
When did they live?		
Name one of their biggest achievements.		

2. Give one example of how these two groups are similar.

   _____

   _____

   _____

3. Give one example of how these two groups are different.

   _____

   _____

   _____

Thinking about my learning

☺ I understand and can do this well.
😐 I understand but I am not confident.
☹ I don't understand and find this difficult.

Learning outcome	☺	😐	☹
Explain who the Vikings were.			
Recall how, why and where the Vikings travelled.			
Describe how the Vikings were ruled.			
Recall what life was like in a Viking village.			
Describe the achievements that the Vikings are known for.			

One thing I learned about how people in Viking times lived is…

_____

_____

One difference between life in the time of the Vikings and life today is…

_____

_____

The best fact I know about the Vikings is…

_____

_____

One thing I would still like to know about the Vikings is…

_____

_____

2 The Age of Discovery and Exploration

What do I already know?

What do you think are good answers to the questions in the speech bubbles? Discuss your answers with some friends. Write your answers in your notebook. Your teacher will ask you to look back at your answers when you have completed the unit.

> What do the words 'discovery' and 'exploration' mean?

> How do you think trade and ideas spread around the world about 1000 years ago?

> What do you think the term 'Golden Age' means?

> What famous explorers have you already studied? Where did they travel to?

> What do you think life was like on board the ship pictured on page 20 of your Student Book?

Things I would like to know about the Age of Discovery and Exploration

_____

_____

_____

Look at this image and answer the questions.

1 How do you think it felt to be a sailor on this voyage to a foreign land?

　

　

2 Why do you think people went on voyages of discovery and exploration?

　

　

3 What goods and weapons do you think the explorers took with them?

　

　

4 Where do you think the explorers were travelling to?

2.1 Before the Age of Discovery and Exploration

Trade and travel in the Middle East

1 Read this source, which is a list of goods traded in Baghdad in the 9th century CE. Organise the goods by completing the table below.

- From China: spices, silk, porcelain, paper, ink, horses, saddles, rhubarb
- From the Byzantines: silver and gold vessels, coins, medicines, cloth, slaves, experts in water engineering and farming
- From Arabia: horses, camels, animal skins
- From North Africa: leopards and black falcons
- From Yemen: cloaks, giraffes, armour, indigo
- From Egypt: donkeys, fine cloth
- From Central Asia: slaves, armour, helmets, grapes, sugar
- From Persia: plums, soft woollen coats, honey, fruit drinks, glass

Animals	Goods	New ideas and technology

2 Why do you think these goods were popular in the 9th century CE? Explain your answer.

_____

_____

_____

_____

3 Answer these questions about trade and travel in the Middle East.

   a Why was Baghdad important for trade in the 9th century CE?

_____

_____

   b How did the traded goods make their way to Europe from the Middle East?

_____

_____

Progress in the Middle East

'Before the Age of Discovery and Exploration, people in the Middle East made great progress in science, medicine, engineering, mathematics and astronomy.'
Do you agree with this statement? Explain your ideas.

_____

_____

_____

_____

_____

2.2 Why was there an Age of Discovery and Exploration?

Exploration and trade

1. When did the Age of Discovery and Exploration begin?

   _____

2. Why did people go on explorations at this time?

   _____

The Ottoman Empire

Research the Ottoman Empire and write your findings in the table.

Date(s) Geographical location Capital city	Area and countries in the Ottoman Empire
Write six important facts about the Ottoman Empire. 1 _____ 2 _____ 3 _____ 4 _____ 5 _____ 6 _____	

Challenge

In your notebook write a summary of the reasons why the Ottoman Empire grew at this time. State which reasons you think were the most important and explain why.

A new age of learning

Read this statement and answer the questions.

> The Ottomans began to take over more and more land. Many scholars in the Middle East decided to move away. The people who moved were some of the world's best writers, musicians, astronomers, architects, artists, scientists and mathematicians. Most of these scholars settled in Italy. They set up schools and colleges in cities such as Florence and Padua. They brought with them manuscripts and books written in Ancient Greece and Rome, as well as their own knowledge. Much of the ancient knowledge had been forgotten in Europe. Europeans realised that many of their own ideas were wrong.

1 What caused the 'new age of learning'?

_____

2 What impacts did the Middle Eastern scholars have on the people in Europe?

_____

_____

_____

3 What do you think was the most important impact or change? Explain your ideas.

_____

_____

_____

4 What impact did the growth of the Ottoman Empire have on scholars in the Middle East?

_____

_____

2.3a Voyages of discovery and exploration

The history of exploration

1 These important facts about the history of exploration are mixed up.
Draw a line to match each date and person with the correct fact.

| 1416 CE Prince Henry of Portugal | | Tried to reach the Far East and instead landed in North America. |

| 1488 CE Bartolomeu Dias | | Landed in the West Indies. |

| 1492 CE Christopher Columbus | | Founded a school of map-making and navigation. |

| 1497 CE John Cabot | | Became the first European to sail around Africa and land in India. |

| 1498 CE Vasco da Gama | | His ships were the first to sail around the world. |

| 1519–1522 CE Ferdinand Magellan | | Became the first European to sail into the Indian Ocean. |

2 Answer these questions about the history of exploration.

a Why did Prince Henry have such an important role in encouraging exploration in Europe?

_____

_____

b Which two developments in technology helped explorers?

_____

_____

c What goods did Portuguese explorers bring back to Europe?

_____

_____

Celebrating exploration

The Monument to the Discoveries was built in 1960 on the bank of the Tagus River in Lisbon, Portugal. From this spot, Portuguese ships set off to explore and trade with India, Africa and the Far East. The monument is shaped like a ship's sails and features some of Portugal's best-known explorers, such as Vasco da Gama and Bartolomeu Dias. A statue of Prince Henry is at the front.

Design your own monument to celebrate the lives of the explorers you have read about and studied.

2.3b Voyages of discovery and exploration

Explorers

There are two fact files on these pages. One is for Vasco da Gama and the other is for an explorer who came from your country or region. Do some research and complete the fact files in as much detail as possible.

All about Vasco da Gama	
Born	
Died	
Nationality	

Interesting facts about the explorations of Vasco da Gama	Countries discovered
Problems Vasco da Gama and his crew faced	How Vasco da Gama was significant to exploration

Local history study

Complete this fact file for the explorer you have chosen. Find a picture of your chosen explorer to cut out and stick on to your fact file.

All about _____	(Stick your picture in this space.)
Born	
Died	
Nationality	

Interesting facts about the explorations of this explorer	Countries discovered

Problems this explorer and crew faced	How this explorer was significant to exploration

2 The Age of Discovery and Exploration

2.4 What was life like at sea?

A caravel

A caravel was a type of ship that was used for exploration.

1   Look at the numbered phrases in the box. Label the caravel with the correct numbers.

1 two large sails	5 rudder	8 brightly coloured flags
2 the captain's cabin	6 the 'crow's nest'	9 platform for guns
3 brightly painted	7 smaller sail to help the ship sail into the wind	10 storage for weapons and trade goods
4 anchor		

2   List the reasons why many explorers used a caravel to travel the world.

_____

_____

_____

Life on board a caravel

Write a newspaper article about Ferdinand Magellan's journey around the world. You could include an image of the ship he travelled on or a map showing where he travelled. Include information about:

- Magellan's journey around the world
- the caravel
- conditions on board the ship
- problems the explorers faced on the journey.

The Daily Explorer

2.5 What was the Renaissance?

The printing press

Answer these questions about the invention of the printing press.

1 When was the printing press invented?

   _____

   _____

2 What did this new invention do?

   _____

   _____

3 How did the printing press help communicate new ideas during the Renaissance?

   _____

   _____

4 What new ideas did the printing press help to spread?

   _____

   _____

A Golden Age

Complete the essay. Explain whether you think life changed during the Renaissance. Each section has been started for you.

 **Introduction:** Tell the reader a bit about the Renaissance, including when and where it took place. Remember to include dates and the names of the countries you have studied.

Reasons: Tell the reader all the things that changed. Think about the achievements of the Renaissance, new discoveries and inventions. Say why these achievements were important. Write a sentence or two for each reason.

Conclusion: Was the Renaissance a 'golden age of discovery'? Say what you think.

Title: The Renaissance period was a 'golden age' for science, literature and discovery. Do you agree?

The Renaissance began _____

_____

_____

_____

During the Renaissance many things changed, for example, _____

_____

_____

_____

_____

_____

In conclusion, I think that _____

_____

_____

2 Thinking about my learning

The Age of Discovery and Exploration

Find your answers to the questions in speech bubbles on page 20 at the beginning of the unit. Use a different colour to add to your answers or rewrite them. Include any new information you have learned while studying this unit.

Timeline of the Age of Discovery and Exploration

Choose eight important dates from the Age of Discovery and Exploration. Write them on the timeline in chronological order. Write a sentence to describe what happened on each date.

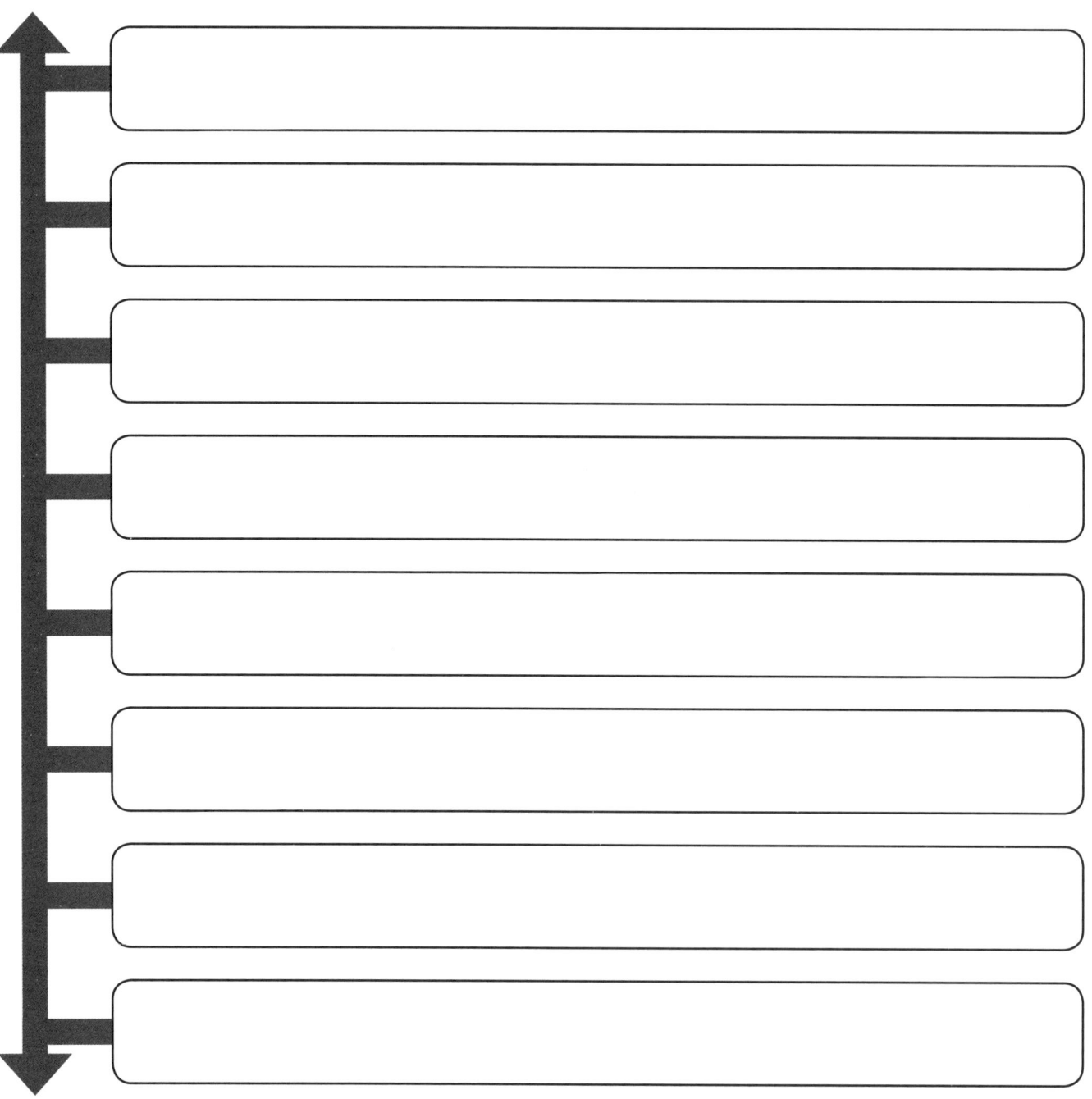

Thinking about my learning

☺ I understand and can do this well.
😐 I understand but I am not confident.
☹ I don't understand and find this difficult.

Learning outcome	☺	😐	☹
Recall what the 'Golden Age' means.			
Explain how trade and ideas spread before the Age of Discovery and Exploration.			
Analyse why there was an Age of Discovery and Exploration.			
Recall some of the key voyages at this time.			
Describe what life was like on a ship at this time.			

One thing I learned about the Age of Discovery and Exploration is…

_____

_____

One difference between the Age of Discovery and Exploration and today is…

_____

_____

The best fact I know about the Age of Discovery and Exploration is…

_____

_____

One thing I would still like to know about the Age of Discovery and Exploration is…

_____

_____

3 The Tudors

What do I already know?

What do you think are good answers to the questions in the speech bubbles? Discuss your answers with some friends. Write your answers in your notebook. Your teacher will ask you to look back at your answers when you have completed the unit.

> Do you know of any famous Tudor kings and queens?

> When and where did the Tudor kings and queens rule?

> What was it like to live in Tudor times?

> What did a Tudor town look like?

> Where did the Tudors begin to explore and trade?

Things I would like to know about the Tudors

_____

_____

_____

Look at this image and answer the questions.

1 Who is this?

_____

2 What do you think her role is?

_____

_____

3 How is she dressed? What does this tell us about her?

_____

_____

4 Why do you think this portrait was painted?

_____

_____

5 What can we learn about this person from her portrait?

_____

3.1 Who were the Tudor kings and queens?

The Tudors take control

In 1485 CE, a new family of rulers, the Tudors, became the ruling royal family of England. The Tudors ruled England for the next 118 years, until 1603 CE.

Draw your own version of the Tudor family tree in the box.

My family tree

The Tudor family tree has three generations – grandparents, parents and children. Work with an adult to create a family tree for your own family or a fictional family, with at least three generations. Draw your family tree on a piece of paper or in your notebook.

Henry VIII's children

1 Use reference books or the Internet to complete this table about the children of Henry VIII.

	Edward VI	**Mary I**	**Elizabeth I**
Born			
Died			
Dates ruled			
Parents			
Spouse(s)			
Interesting fact 1			
Interesting fact 2			
Interesting fact 3			

2 Henry's youngest child, Edward, ruled first when Henry died. Why?

_____

_____

_____

3.2 Who was who in Tudor society?

Who was who?

Match each description with the correct word.

| Gentlemen |
| Citizens |
| Yeomen |
| Labourers |

- They were farmers. They either owned land or rented land from a gentleman.
- Many were merchants who made money from buying and selling goods such as wool, jewellery, food or cloth. They lived in towns.
- They were poor. Most lived in the countryside and worked on a farm for a yeoman. Some worked as servants.
- They were the richest, most powerful people in Tudor society. They owned large areas of land and lived in huge houses in the countryside.

Tudor society

1 Look at the following images. Write five words to describe each image. Then answer the question about each image.

A

1 _____

2 _____

3 _____

4 _____

5 _____

Who do you think lived in this house?

_____

B

1 _____
2 _____
3 _____
4 _____
5 _____

Who do you think lived in this house?

_____

C

1 _____
2 _____
3 _____
4 _____
5 _____

Who do you think this picture shows?

_____

2 Which image do you think is the most useful to a historian? Explain your answer.

_____

_____

Challenge

Compare Elizabeth I with a famous monarch from today. Write a summary (200–300 words) in your notebook explaining all the similarities and differences. Think about where both monarchs rule or ruled, the length of their reign and some successes or failures they experienced. Be prepared to share your summary with the class.

3.3 Tudor towns

Tudor towns

1 Look at your Student Book pages 42–43 to remind yourself of the important features of a Tudor town. Then write a label for each part of the picture.

1	4	7
2	5	8
3	6	9

2 How is the Tudor town different from where you live? Complete the table.

	Tudor town	**Where I live**
Describe the place in one sentence.		
What can you do there?		
Is disease common? Why?		
What are the buildings made from?		
What are the homes like?		
What technology can you see to help everyday life?		
What problems or dangers are there?		

3.4 Fun and games in Tudor times

Change over time

The ways in which people have fun today have changed since Tudor times. Write a report about how fun and games have changed.

 Write a paragraph about fun and games in Tudor times. Write another paragraph about how we have fun today. Explain why the ways in which people have fun have changed over time.

In Tudor times, people had fun in different ways, for example…

_____

_____

_____

_____

Today, we have fun by…

_____

_____

_____

_____

The ways in which people have fun have changed over time. For example, …

_____

_____

_____

_____

Fun and games in Tudor times

1 Think of 12 words linked to fun and games in Tudor times. Write the words below.

_____   _____   _____

_____   _____   _____

_____   _____   _____

_____   _____   _____

2 Use your words to create a wordsearch puzzle. Ask another student to solve your wordsearch.

3.5 What were Tudor schools like?

The school day

Life as a child in Tudor times was different from children's lives today!

1. Colour in the sections of the clock to show your normal school day including when you eat, sleep, study, play, and so on. Use a different colour for each type of activity. Colour in the key to show what each colour means. There is space to add two more activities if you wish.

6.00 a.m.	Day starts with Latin grammar
8.00 a.m.	Mathematics
10.00 a.m.	Greek grammar
12:00 noon	Lunch: bread, cheese, beef, dried fruit
1.00 p.m.	Essays
2.00 p.m.	Religious studies
3.00 p.m.	English
4.00 p.m.	Homework time
4.45 p.m.	Prayers
5.00 p.m.	Home

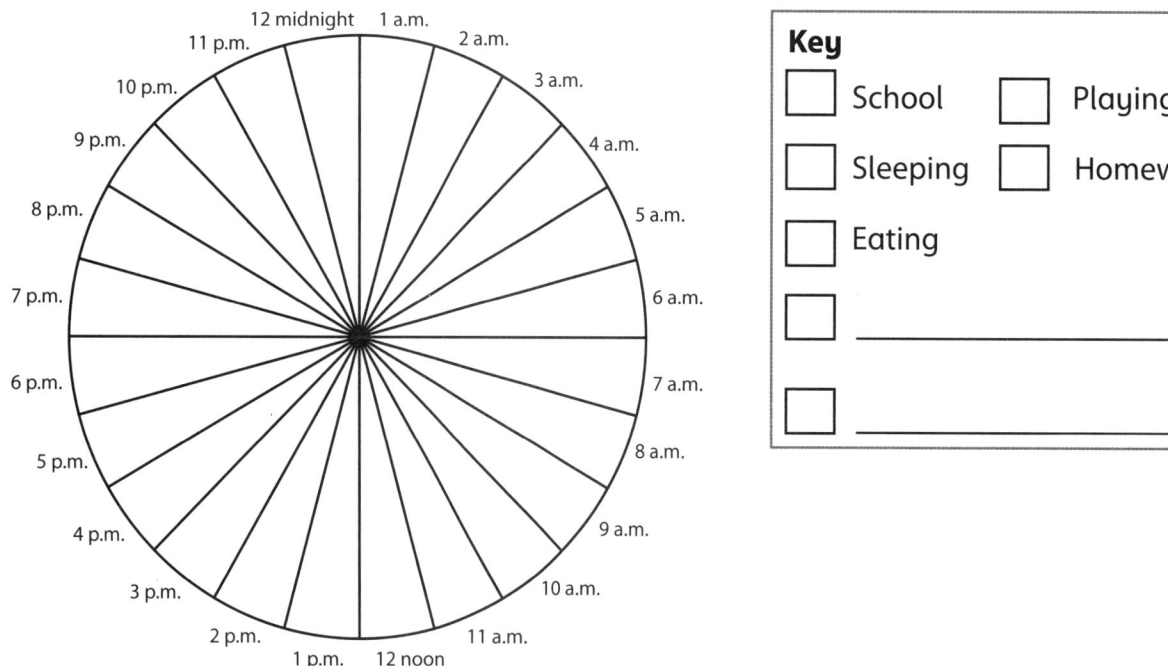

Key
- [ ] School
- [ ] Sleeping
- [ ] Eating
- [ ] Playing
- [ ] Homework
- [ ] _____
- [ ] _____

2. How was a Tudor child's day different from your day? Write three sentences explaining your ideas.

_____

_____

_____

_____

Tudor school report

You are an adviser to King Henry VIII. Write a government report to tell the king about schools in Tudor England. Use the headings below to help you structure your report.

A description of schools in Tudor England:

_____
_____
_____
_____

These are the differences between education for the rich and education for the poor:

_____
_____
_____
_____
_____

These are my ideas to improve schools:

_____
_____
_____
_____
_____
_____
_____
_____

3.6 What do Tudor portraits tell us?

Write a guidebook for the gallery where these portraits are on display.

First write an introduction with information about Queen Elizabeth I.

Then write about each portrait. Include when the portrait was painted and what each symbol means. Look at the complete portraits in your Student Book to help you.

Introduction: _____
_____
_____
_____
_____

Date painted: _____   Elizabeth's age: _____

Meaning of the symbols:

Headdress _____

Pearls _____

Pelican _____

Gold jewellery and fan _____

Colours of clothing _____

Tudor roses _____

What does this portrait tell us about Elizabeth?
_____
_____

Date painted: _____ Elizabeth's age: _____

Meaning of the symbols:

Ships _____

Globe _____

Pearls _____

Crown _____

Black clothing _____

Make-up _____

What does this portrait tell us about Elizabeth?

_____

_____

Date painted: _____ Elizabeth's age: _____

Meaning of the symbols:

Jewels _____

Long hair _____

Flowers _____

Eyes and ears on the cloak _____

Rainbow _____

Snake _____

What does this portrait tell us about Elizabeth?

_____

_____

3 Thinking about my learning

The Tudors

Find your answers to the questions in speech bubbles on page 36 at the beginning of the unit. Use a different colour to add to your answers or rewrite them. Include any new information you have learned while studying this unit.

Remembering the Tudors

Some buildings that the Tudors built still stand today. Millions of tourists visit these Tudor buildings hoping to learn what life was like during Tudor times.

Hampton Court Palace, just outside London, England. This was the main palace of one of the most famous Tudor kings, Henry VIII.

Research three Tudor landmarks that you would like to visit. Explain why.

_____

_____

_____

_____

_____

Local history study

Research three historical landmarks in your own country. Explain in your notebook why you would like to visit them.

Thinking about my learning

☺ I understand and can do this well.
😐 I understand but I am not confident.
☹ I don't understand and find this difficult.

Learning outcome	☺	😐	☹
Explain what it was like to live in Tudor times.			
Describe what a Tudor town looked like.			
Recall why and where the Tudors began to explore and trade.			
Explain how England changed in Tudor times.			

One thing I learned about how the Tudors lived is…

_____

_____

One difference between life in Tudor times and life today is…

_____

_____

The best fact I know about the Tudors is…

_____

_____

One thing I would still like to know about the Tudors is…

_____

_____

4 The story of London

What do I already know?

What do you think are good answers to the questions in the speech bubbles? Discuss your answers with some friends. Write your answers in your notebook. Your teacher will ask you to look back at your answers when you have completed the unit.

> Where is London?

> Can you think of reasons why London is so famous?

> What important events have happened in London's history?

> What was the London plague?

> What was the Great Fire of London?

> What famous buildings are in London?

> Which famous people live or have lived in London?

Things I would like to know about London

_____

_____

Look at this image and answer the questions.

1 Which city is this? Which country is it in? What famous buildings or landmarks can you see?

   _____

   _____

2 What famous events might have happened in this building?

   _____

   _____

3 How might this building have changed over time?

   _____

   _____

4 What famous residents might have lived here?

   _____

   _____

4.1 Ancient London

The location of London

True or false?

1 Put ✓ in the box next to the statements that are correct. Put ✗ in the box next to the statements that are incorrect.

    a The Romans invaded Britain in 430 CE. ☐

    b The Romans built a bridge across the River Thames, where London is located today. ☐

    c In about 50 CE, the Romans decided that London was an excellent place to build a salt mine. ☐

    d The River Thames was shallow enough for larger trading ships. ☐

    e The Romans thought London would be safe from attacks by foreign tribes because it was inland. ☐

    f The Romans believed London was a good place from which to build roads to every part of Britain. ☐

    g When the Romans decided to settle, the first thing they built was the forum. ☐

    h The Romans called the town Londinium, and we know it today as London. ☐

2 Rewrite the statements that are incorrect.

_____

_____

_____

_____

_____

Ancient London

1 Create your own timeline of the history of ancient London. Include six events in London's history from the invasion of the Romans to the reign of the Anglo-Saxon King Alfred. Make sure you include the date of each event.

2 Why do you think the Romans left London in 410 CE? Explain your reasons.

_____

_____

_____

_____

_____

4.2 London in the Middle Ages

The Tower of London

Create a fact file about the Tower of London.

Tower of London fact file	
Date built Size Height Number of towers	History of the Tower of London
Drawing of the Tower of London	
	Famous people who lived (or were kept prisoner) here
What is the Tower of London used for today?	

Local history study

Research an important building or landmark where you live that was built around the same time as the Tower of London. Write your findings in your notebook. Be prepared to share your findings with the class.

London in the Middle Ages

Look at the larger version of this map in your Student Book and answer the questions.

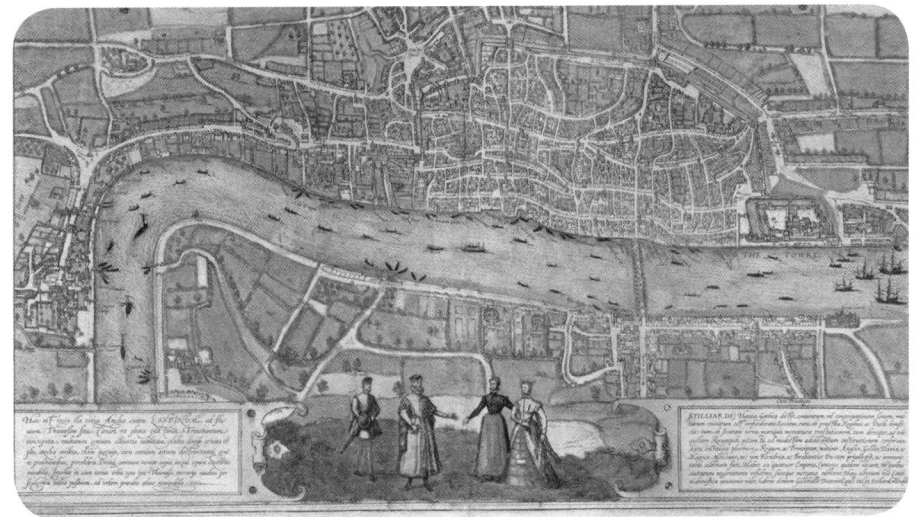

A map of London from the 1500s CE. By this time, the population of London had grown to about 60 000.

1 Why did people move to London during the Middle Ages?

_____

_____

2 London was surrounded by fields. What were these used for?

_____

_____

3 What was the River Thames used for in the Middle Ages?

_____

_____

4 How do you think London has changed since this map was drawn?

_____

_____

5 How useful is this map to a historian studying the Middle Ages?

_____

4.3a How did the Great Fire change London?

Research the Great Fire

Find out what caused the Great Fire of London, the damage it did and how London was rebuilt. Use books or the Internet for your research. Complete the table by writing the most important five facts for each topic.

Causes of the Great Fire of London	1	
	2	
	3	
	4	
	5	
Damage done by the fire	1	
	2	
	3	
	4	
	5	
How London was rebuilt	1	
	2	
	3	
	4	
	5	

The Great Fire

Samuel Pepys kept a diary of what he saw during the fire. He watched the fire from across the River Thames. Imagine you lived next door to Samuel Pepys. Write an entry in your diary describing what the Great Fire of London was like.

| **16 September 1666** |
| Thursday |

Dear Diary,

What an exciting and scary couple of days it has been here in London. _____

_____

People believe the fire started because _____

_____

There are many different reasons why the fire spread so quickly. _____

_____

_____

_____

The fire destroyed _____

_____

_____

The fire stopped because _____

_____

_____

The rebuilding of London will begin _____

_____

_____

4.3b How did the Great Fire change London?

Life after the Great Fire of London

 Write an essay explaining how life in London changed after the Great Fire. In your essay give reasons for your answer, showing you have thought about the short-term and long-term consequences.

Title: How much did life in London change after the Great Fire?

The Great Fire of London was an important event in London's history because…

_____

_____

_____

London changed during and after the Great Fire because…

_____

_____

_____

However, some things in London stayed the same. For example,…

_____

_____

_____

Overall, I think…

_____

_____

_____

Christopher Wren

Using your research skills, create your own fact file about Christopher Wren. Find out about his job and how he changed London after the Great Fire.

All about Christopher Wren
Age at the time of the Great Fire _____   Nationality _____   Job _____
Three ways in which Christopher Wren changed London   1   2   3

4.4 The largest city in the world

Victorian London

These two pictures show the differences between rich and poor in London in Victorian times. They were taken at about the same time, only a few miles apart, in different areas of London.

1 Compare the two images.

   a What can we learn about life for the poorest people in London at this time?

   _____
   _____
   _____

   b What can we learn about life for wealthy people in London at this time?

   _____
   _____
   _____

2 How useful are these images to a historian learning about Victorian London?

   _____
   _____
   _____

3 The year is 1898. London is the capital of Queen Victoria's empire. Write a newspaper article about Victoria's London. Your article should include information on: the Industrial Revolution, trade and industry, famous buildings, how London changed during Queen Victoria's reign.

Empire Express

4.5 London at war

The Blitz

Imagine you are a reporter in October 1940 and this picture will be on the front of tomorrow's newspaper. Write your headline in the box next to the picture. Then write an opening paragraph for the newspaper article. Tell the people of London what has happened.

Headline:

Rebuilding London

Here are five changes made in London after the Blitz.

1 **New buildings:** Much of bombed London had to be rebuilt. A series of high-rise apartments (known as flats) were built.

2 **Moving out:** When the war ended, the government revealed plans to relocate Londoners from poor-quality or bombed-out housing. About 20–30 miles from London, 10 new towns were built.

3 **Industrial changes:** Industries such as car-making and aircraft making, engineering and electronics went into decline, while banking, tourism and construction flourished.

4 **Moving in:** Many thousands of immigrants from the West Indies, Pakistan, India, Africa and China moved into London.

5 **Population:** London's population began to rise again as people moved into the city looking for work. In the early years of the 21st century, the population was about 8 million.

1 Which of these changes do you think had the biggest impact on people's everyday lives? Use the pyramid to rank the importance of these changes. Write the number of the most important change at the top and the number of the least important change at the bottom.

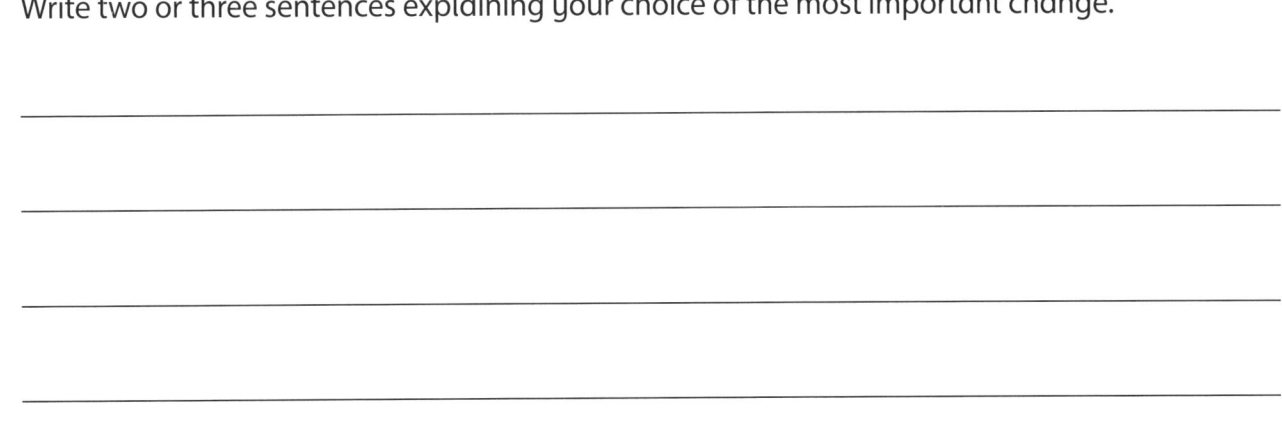

2 Write two or three sentences explaining your choice of the most important change.

_____

_____

_____

_____

4 Thinking about my learning

London

Find your answers to the questions in speech bubbles on page 52 at the beginning of the unit. Use a different colour to add to your answers or rewrite them. Include any new information you have learned while studying this unit.

London today

Use books and the Internet to make a list of five facts about London since 2000.

1 _____

2 _____

3 _____

4 _____

5 _____

Local history study

Use books and the Internet to make a list of five facts about the capital city of the country where you live. Write your answers in your notebook.

Thinking about my learning

☺ I understand and can do this well.
😐 I understand but I am not confident.
☹ I don't understand and find this difficult.

Learning outcome	☺	😐	☹
Explain who first settled in London and why.			
Describe how and why London grew so rapidly.			
Recall how plagues, fires and invasions had a major impact on London.			
Explain the history behind some of London's most famous buildings.			
Summarise how London has changed and continues to develop.			

One thing I learned about London is…

_____

_____

One difference between life in the early days of London and life today is…

_____

_____

The best fact I know about London is…

_____

_____

One thing I would still like to know about London is…

_____

_____

Glossary

Using your own words, explain what these words mean.

Blitz

craftsperson

explorer

family tree

fire-break

Industrial Revolution

merchant

Glossary

Middle Ages

monarch

Henry VIII    Elizabeth I

navigator

plague

portrait

rebuild

Renaissance

scholar

society

symbol

Tudor

warrior